Ignore the Guy, Get the Guy
The Art of No Contact

A *WOMAN'S* Survival Guide to:
Mastering a Breakup and Taking Back Her Power

Written By
Leslie Braswell

Cover Designed by 99Designs

DISCLAIMER AND/OR LEGAL NOTICES

The information presented and contained herein represents the view of the author as of the date of this publication. The author reserves the right to change her opinions based on new information at any time.

This material is general dating advice only and is not intended to be a substitute for professional, medical or psychological advice and/or counseling.
No part of this book may be reproduced in any form or by any electronic or mechanical means including information storage and retrieval systems without written permission from the author.

Acknowledgements

To my Devine God that makes all things possible. To my children who are simply amazing, my source of strength. And to my mother for being the strongest influence in my life.

Table of Contents

Intuition...a girls best friend

INTRODUCTION

Just about every woman has been through a breakup at some point during her life. Maybe your boyfriend just broke up with you and now all you want to do is crawl in bed and tell the world you're out of the country. It doesn't matter if you dated for three months or three years. Life as you knew it drastically changed and the man you cared a great deal about is no longer a part of your reality.

You need to know that every woman has the ability to reverse a breakup. It doesn't matter what the circumstances are as long as you play your cards right from the beginning. Know that you can completely change the outcome. You've probably known at least one friend who went a little crazy after a breakup. Maybe you were that girl. In my book you'll learn why you should stop right now in your tracks, if you are in any way trying to convince your ex why he needs you. This book will show you what you can do to shift the power back in your favor.

When I use the word *ignore* or *no contact* I'm not using them in a rude, disrespectful or even a childish way. You've probably heard the term, "Silence speaks louder than words." Many women believe the best way to get their point across is to verbally express their feelings. However, after a breakup, expressing your feelings is the last approach you should take because during this time… a man doesn't want to hear it. There is nothing you can say that will change his mind.

The next few chapters will show you how to manage your emotions and keep calm with your dignity and pride in check. How to create a plan to put your life back on track without wasting precious weeks, months or years holding on to the past, and answers to all of your breakup questions. I also tell you the reaction a man is expecting from you and how you can deprive him of the ego boost so many women before you have provided.

We all invest in our education to enhance our knowledge of a subject. *And knowledge is power.* We should all learn the same about a breakup. Have a plan in place. Remember you are the one who controls you and only you. Years and months down the road you'll be glad you took the time to teach yourself this skill. *And it is a skill!* Controlling your emotions takes discipline and willpower. There's no way around it...a breakup hurts like hell. It is unfortunate it is not a subject taught in school. And one point I believe all women would agree on is, when it comes to dating we need help. Lots and lots of help.

This book was written for women who are overwhelmed by a breakup and need a survival guide to get through the next few weeks or months like a pro. This book gives advice on how to keep yourself in check, so you can get your love life back to the place it needs to be. Open, ready and willing to receive love.

If you've ever let yourself fall to pieces, cried, begged and groveled to a man to take you back after a breakup, or if you have ever sought closure, then you've never learned *the art* or *the power of no contact.* Now is the time to learn it, live it and master it.

Handle a breakup the wrong way and you will ruin the chance of a reconciliation. However, handle it the right way and Mr. Ex will question himself for ever letting you getaway. Always remember the power you possess as a woman still reigns supreme. *You have everything a man wants and always will.*

What is your goal? To be able to function? To get through each day? To move on and forget about Mr. Ex? *Or would you like to lure him back by your side?* Stand your ground now, play your cards right and reap the rewards later. Remember to always think of your long-term goal and plan backwards.

Let's begin!

————————

Pour yourself a drink, put on some lipstick, and pull yourself together.

Elizabeth Taylor

————————

CHAPTER ONE

WHY NO CONTACT WORKS

In a perfect world, when a man breaks up with us, what we would do is gently smile and agree with the breakup. We would kindly wish him well and exit the premises immediately with our head held high. No hard feelings and no ill will. We would handle ourselves the same if he broke up by phone. If he did it by text we simply would take the high road and choose not to reply.

That makes me laugh hysterically because in the aftermath of a breakup your reaction is anything but kind, warm and rational. Act in a mature way? *Forget about it*! Your world as you knew it just changed with a few simple words that hold a great deal of meaning.

If you were just informed of the death of your best friend, chances are you wouldn't handle it without showing signs of emotion, now would you? *Of course not!* The feelings associated with the death of a loved one are equivalent to what one experiences post breakup. Of course, the difference is there is a living, breathing being existing in the world you can't bring back. Your relationship died and you're mourning the loss. It's perfectly normal to be upset.

However how you handle a breakup on the outside is what separates the women from the girls. Even die-hard *Rules* girls who have perfected the dos and don'ts of dating have let an unexpected breakup shake them to the core.

You'll first analyze the relationship, specifically the last month and go over and over in your mind trying to figure out what exactly you did wrong. You rationalize maybe you weren't available enough. You begin to think you should have cooked his favorite meals more. Maybe you should have participated more in his hobbies. You'll rack your brain trying to understand something that's impossible to understand.

After all, the two of you were happy, weren't you? If you could only talk to him... But no, he's not answering calls. Text messages are not being responded to, which is making you sink down into a bottomless pit of despair.

SILENCE IS A WOMAN'S BEST FRIEND

Immediately after a breakup the hardest part is controlling your emotions. Which is why silence is golden...it camouflages your emotions. It's perfectly fine to fall to pieces... *just not in front of Mr. Ex.* Stay calm, grounded, don't cry, beg, plead or grovel for him to take you back. This behavior may sound pathetic, but this is the exact approach some women take after a breakup.

By keeping your emotions under control you keep your power right where it belongs. **With you!** You may argue it may be wrong to hide your emotions and that you're not being your authentic self, but keep in mind men hide their emotions every day. That's what separates men from women. Our emotions. And men are experts at reading our emotions and using them to their advantage *(which makes you an easy target).* If you display all of your emotions you are showing all of your cards and losing the game before it even begins.

15

I am sure you've heard the old saying, "Men think with their penis, not their brain?" After a break up you are thinking with your heart...not *your* brain. Be smart and think logically during emotional times. Always use your logic to outsmart men. *Go silent so he can't possibly tell what you are thinking. Leave him guessing.*

By not allowing him to know what you're thinking, you transfer those feelings of insecurity and rejection he has made you feel, back to him. **No Contact** makes him perk up and actually take another look at you. Men want what they can't have. And you have to make him feel you're no longer his.

A STRONG WOMAN STEALS THE SHOW

A strong woman knows how to take care of her and the life that she has created. More importantly, she knows her mind. She doesn't allow drama in her life. And she doesn't allow a man to make her messy. She knows her value and self-worth and has the confidence and self-esteem to back it up. She's with a man because she *wants* to be, not because she *needs* to be. She knows in advance if a man walks out of her life, it's his loss. She acknowledges having a man around is a bonus, not a necessity and is perfectly capable of taking care of herself without one. And men are attracted to women that possess the ability to walk away from a relationship, as bees are to honey.

When you immediately spring into fix it mode trying to repair a relationship, you're falling for his game. He's expecting you to call and text him at all hours of the day and night professing your undying love. This is what the "hard to get man" is accustomed to. And guess what? He's losing respect for you each time he sees your name pop up on his phone. He's thinking he has a front row seat to the best drama show on earth and you're the star of the show. Your actions are telling him he won't have to break a sweat to win you back because you're doing all of the hard work for him.

Too many women fall in love and without realizing it, unknowingly, begin to give too much of themselves in the process. Maybe you were hard to get in the beginning, let him chase you like a lion chases its prey and then...*he caught you*. Maybe your only fault is being *too nice* and *too available*. And men believe women that are too nice and too available are not only thirsty for love, but are completely dehydrated. Most women do not even realize they are doing this until it is too late.

It's only natural to want to make the man you love happy. But when you give too much of yourself, is when a relationship unravels. You've lost his interest. You're no longer the sexy siren that caught his attention. You became the woman that gave too freely, arranged her life around his, answered the phone when it rang, and gave it your all only to be left in shock when he became bored, or met someone else who provides him with the thrill of the chase. It's a vicious never-ending cycle.

HOW TO PREVENT A MAN FROM LOSING INTEREST

If you never lose interest in yourself chances are he will never lose interest in you. By setting your standards so high, he constantly has to work to meet them. By knowing your boundaries and by refusing to accept any bad behavior. *By respecting yourself so much he will place you right where you belong...on a pedestal.* You accomplish this task by never allowing him to believe, you've been caught.

With most men it's about making the conquest. They want to know that they can have you. Once they get you, they don't need to prove anything so they move on to the next woman who thinks they're handsome, smart, charming and perfect. The biggest myth about relationships is that men are afraid of commitment. What men are afraid of is losing the adrenaline rush they get when a new woman believes in her mind he's some fantasy prince charming.

When you have other things going on in your life besides him, he doesn't feel suffocated or chained to a tree like dog, so always strive to keep your life a fulfilled one. You should view a man as a topping to an already great dessert. The dessert is fine on its own but it's always a bit sweeter with all the extras.

EMAILS, TEXT MESSAGES, AND SOCIAL MEDIA

Technology has made it nearly impossible for women to remain a little mysterious and even harder on women to handle a breakup, because there are simply too many avenues of communication. Keyboards are readily available right at your delicate fingertips to express emotions you feel the need to get off your chest...*immediately*! And it's true nobody can text faster than a pissed off woman.

Women are mostly defined as creatures of habit. Throw an unexpected breakup in the mix and you fall to pieces. While you are left devastated over the breakup, Mr. Ex is one-step ahead of you. He has had plenty of time to plan and prepare his exit well in advance of informing you of his decision to do so. This is why he is handling the breakup like a champ... he has had ample time to prepare himself mentally and to detach himself emotionally.

WHY WOMEN LOSE THE BATTLE OF THE BREAKUP

Because women fall apart when they're not mentally prepared and are caught off guard... *just as if you were notified about a loved one's death.* It shocks you! By the time your brain has registered exactly what has transpired, you immediately want to get everything out in the open. This is also a perfect example of what not to do.

By going silent immediately after a breakup, you handle it the right way from the beginning. *No Contact* accomplishes two goals: The first is to recover from the breakup and move on to Mr. Right, which gives you an opportunity to begin your life with a fresh new start. It also tells Mr. Ex that you are secure with who you are, and perfectly competent enough to handle your own life.

The second is to give Mr. Ex space and time so that he has ample opportunity to wonder what you are thinking. By controlling your emotions, you regain your power from the start, by making the decision to not initiate any form of contact. **No contact** hides the fact that you may be falling apart. Regardless of your intent, implementing *No Contact* accomplishes either goal you desire to accomplish.

There is absolutely no need to make an announcement to the world, or to Mr. Ex, for that matter, of your intention of not speaking with him again. **Starting *No Contact* means you are quietly taking a step back and will make no effort whatsoever to contact him during this time.**

This includes, but is not limited to, phone calls, text messages, running into Mr. Ex, and definitely no ex sex! It means you are going to accept the breakup for what is, regardless if you have closure or not and quietly vanish from radar. Women that truly understand their self-worth don't pursue men. And a man won't value you, if you immediately go into overdrive to fix a relationship after a breakup.

Just make an agreement with yourself that you will not initiate any form of contact whatsoever. If you believe anything about yourself, believe that you are worth a damned phone call! If you have sent text messages, called, attempted Morse code, emailed him or tried to reach out to him by creating delusional emergencies or any form of communication, stop now before you sink that ship!

NO DAMAGE CONTROL REQUIRED

You need not offer any apology, explanation or excuse for your behavior. You were going through an emotional time, which is only to be expected. It only shows you loved him. By going silent he will slowly forget about all of the negative thoughts and replace them with positives ones.

Oprah Winfrey once said, "Lots of people want to ride with you in the limo, but what you want is someone who will take the bus with you when the limo breaks down." The same can be applied when it comes to relationships. Don't you want a man that can handle not only the good times, but the bad times, too? Rest assured, if he only wants you during the good times, you can be guaranteed he won't be there for you during the bad times. There is a reason why marriage vows include "for better or for worse." Even if you acted in a way that you are not so proud of, a man that truly loves, cares for you and adores you will be more than willing to handle you with delicate gloves when signs of trouble arise. Men are problem solvers by nature. If they want to fix it, the true alpha male will not miss a beat coming up with ways in which he can fix a problem. If he wants you, he will find a way to solve a problem come hell or high water. If he wants you there is nothing that can or will stand in his way of getting you. And if he can't handle you on your bad days, then understand he's not worthy of you on your good ones. Cut this one loose, fast.

TO MAKE HIM MISS YOU

While you were in a relationship with Mr. Ex, he grew accustom to the attention you gave him. There were perks he received from you because the two of you were in an exclusive committed relationship, which included being available to him, answering his calls, text messages, meeting him for dinner and of course great mind-blowing sex.

Now that you are no longer in an exclusive committed relationship, the only way to make him miss what he had is to make him feel your absence from his life. Only when you make him feel the void will he get serious about getting you back and keeping you all to himself. **If you stay in contact with him from the beginning of the breakup, you fail to make him feel the loss of your presence in his life.** *Just like a death.*

I realize ignoring him goes against every fiber of your being, but now more than ever you must show restraint and self-control. When he calls you'll want to respond with lightning speed, but do nothing that gives him the impression you are sitting on pins and needles waiting on his call or text. Let his call go straight to voicemail. Let it be several hours or days before you respond.

If he sends a text, such as "This weather is beautiful," don't respond. It requires no answer. It's a nothing text and requires a nothing response. If he declares by text he "misses you" ignore that as well. He is just stating he misses you; he's not providing you with a plan which puts you both back together. He's not asking for a dinner date. He's not giving you an explanation that brings you comfort and eases your mind. Don't give him a reward just because he's capable of typing words that form a sentence on a keypad. Unless this is a long distance relationship, I bet he could jump in his car and be next to you within twenty-five minutes, if he missed you that much. Show him the silent treatment until he's knocking on your door, making grand gestures and more importantly providing you with a plan that gives you what you need.

If a reconciliation is in the future you have to make him start over... as in from the beginning. He's has to work to get the relationship back to what it was before he sailed it off course. *Yes*, that's right. Let the chase begin. Until then... You're busy with your new life!

By not allowing him to know where you are and what you are thinking you slowly plant the seeds of insecurity and rejection he has made you feel right back to him. And to accomplish this you have to make him feel you are no longer his.

You may say that you believe this is playing games and you're not one to play games. Well, how's that working for you? In a perfect world there would be no need, but this isn't a perfect world. Chances are he has been playing games with you for months, years or longer. Men live for the thrill of the chase. Once he gets you, chances are he may get bored and start chasing someone else. It's a never-ending game, *so learn how to play it and have fun in the process.*

Men don't realize women don't play hard to get when they are in love. Often, men mistake this love for neediness when in fact you're trying to make the relationship work.

Your instincts are screaming at you to communicate. However, to understand **No Contact** doing exactly the opposite of what you want to do is the best course of action to take. If you were 100% available before, take it down to 20%.

Sherry Argov wrote, "Men don't respond to words, they respond to no contact?" Let silence speak volumes for you. Now is the time to let your quiet strength and inner beauty shine. Show him that your life is going forward and functions quite nicely without him. That is when Mr. Ex's head will spin in your direction and he will begin to seek more attention from you. He'll start to wonder what you are up to for a change, instead of the other way around.

This is exactly what you want. You want to change the dynamics of your relationship with him. When he broke up with you, it was his decision that left your heart shattered. You weren't given the opportunity to fix what was broken. But when you take away the emotional control he has over you, **you win!** You now have the opportunity to show him you are no longer his, and when you can do this, it puts his Texas size ego in check.

Now is the perfect time to reestablish the life you had before he walked into your world. Take the time to reflect on the woman you were when the two of you met. If you let yourself go in any way, now is the time to get back to being that woman. Set new, higher goals for yourself and make a plan to accomplish them. That not only elevates your own life to a higher one, but also makes you more attractive to the men around you. And men love women who constantly strive to better themselves.

Dogs never bite me. Just Humans.

MARILYN MONROE

CHAPTER TWO

THE AFTERMATH OF A BREAKUP

Dennis Quaid once said, "When you breakup, your whole identity is shattered. It's like a death." A breakup is something you thought would never happen. Someone that has been a permanent fixture in your life is gone and it's tearing your heart to pieces. Maybe this is the first time, maybe it's the fourth, fifth or sixth. Maybe it's time to get a little pissed off about a man stringing you along for so long.

During the first week take time to mourn the loss of your relationship. It's dead. The relationship as you knew it, is over. Take this time to reflect on how the relationship sailed off course and take ownership of any way in which you contributed to the split.

FIND YOUR SOURCE OF COMFORT

One woman told me after her breakup, there were days the only source of comfort was her relationship with God. The only source of comfort was crawling in bed, in the fetal position, asking God to please wrap his arms around her and give her comfort and strength. Find your source of comfort and look to that source to provide it to you.

The first week of a breakup, depending on how fragile you are, you will probably want to crawl in bed. You may have a hard time functioning. The first few days are the hardest, most painful and mind numbing experience you may have ever gone through in your life.

It's perfectly all right to be sad and cry the first few days. You may not want to leave the house. You're entitled to that. You're life has been turned inside out. It takes some women every ounce of energy they can muster up just to find the strength to get up each morning, put a smile on their face and go through the daily grind. They're numb from pain.

Another approach is to be *proactive*. Realize mentally a breakup is going to hurt like hell for a little while. Make up your mind you're not going to let this disable your happiness for the upcoming weeks, months or longer. Call your friends immediately and schedule lunch or even better a night out.

OUT OF SIGHT, OUT OF MIND

There are a few adjustments you will want to make in your daily life that you grew accustom to when the two of you were a couple. You may have talked on the phone to Mr. Ex, or had conversations through text messages, or phone calls on a daily basis. It's only normal to pray to the phone god, that your phone rings every single minute of the day. You want with all of your heart's desire for the message alert to go off. It's the equivalent of, "You've Got Mail."

If you had a special ring tone selected for Mr. Ex now is the time to assign him a new one...*preferably a dog bark.* Change all of your ring tones so that familiar sound doesn't trigger a memory of him. That way each text message you receive won't bring you disappointment.

The first week will be the perfect time to remove Mr. Ex's photographs and any personal items from sight. Don't be so fast to burn them all, just pack them away for now.

Getting up and dressed will be like a chore you have to force yourself to do. Make a rule before you leave your home that you'll put forth effort to look your best regardless if you want to, or not. Do it as it will make you feel better. And remember this... *Always look hot in case you run in to Mr. Ex!*

Do you remember the scene in *Hope Floats* when Sandra Bullock takes her daughters lunch to school? She was wearing only her pajamas and robe with no make-up, and her hair a mess. Her daughter was humiliated that her mother appeared at school in front of her friends in such a messy state and ignored her. So as hard as it may be you have to get up and get dressed, don't let anyone see you look like death warmed over. You know you're going through a breakup, but the rest of the world is clueless to this fact. Be the beautiful, unique soul God made you to be. Look beautiful and you will feel beautiful.

On a calendar, or on your phone mark one week from the date of last contact with Mr. Ex. On day seven reward yourself with anything you want. Make an appointment to get your hair styled, a pedicure and a manicure... *(All three never hurt a thing)* Lunch with a friend is even better. You may believe you can't get through these days and I'm not telling you it's going to be a walk in the park, but it is doable. I know it may not seem like it now, but soon you'll look back at this time and think "I can't believe I wasted so much of my time down in the dumps."

Some say to delete Mr. Ex's text messages, emails and voicemails immediately. You know, out of sight-out of mind. I'm going to say keep them and let them serve as a reminder of the pain he may have caused you. And always remember this... *love doesn't hurt.*

Elizabeth wrote after three days of not hearing from her boyfriend of two years he finally sent a text message breaking up with her. She said she wished now she would have never responded, but at the time she was distraught and very emotional. She sent several text messages telling him she loved him and wanted to try to work out any problems they were having. He never responded. She kept those text messages not to revisit the pain, but to let them serve as a reminder that after everything they had shared not only did he end their relationship by text, but also that he couldn't even take the time to reply to one.

Some of the messages and voicemails may bring you a small amount of comfort for the time being. It may be hard to look at an empty inbox. If it makes you feel better keep those old messages and voicemails...*for now.* You'll know when the time is right to delete them permanently. Use any means necessary to get through this first week. Each week thereafter will get easier.

Continue to set on your calendar a reminder for two weeks of *No Contact*, three, and four and so on. When you are able to check off that you made it through another week without dialing his number, you'll feel a sense of pride and accomplishment. Eventually you won't need to set a reminder.

UNDERSTAND WHY YOU'RE TAKING IT SO HARD

One of the major reasons a breakup is hard to go through is because of the loss of feelings associated with being in a relationship. *Being loved.* Everyone wants to feel loved. That feeling doesn't leave just because Mr. Ex did. What so many women confuse is being told they are loved and actually feeling loved. You want to know there is someone in the world that cares for your well-being, that cares you're alive and a person you feel connected to.

What makes a breakup hurt so immensely is the feeling of love Mr. Ex gave you, you aren't giving to yourself. The confidence you derived from the feelings of being adored and cherished are no longer your reality.

Ever notice how 'What the hell' is always the right answer?

CHAPTER THREE

THE EMOTIONAL ROLLER COASTER RIDE

If you know in advance the highs, lows, twists and turns of the emotions you're experiencing, it makes it a lot easier to handle them. If you anticipate and expect the feelings you are having you'll deal with the array of emotions you're experiencing in a logical way. We only handle unexpected situations poorly because we are simply unprepared.

The most intimate and loving relationships can cause the most emotional turmoil. The range of emotions you experience vary from one hour to the next. You experience fear, sadness, resentment, anger and many other conflicting emotions after a breakup. What's important is that you handle your emotions and not allow them to handle you.

We allow ourselves to be caught up in drama. You're angry with Mr. Ex for not wanting what you want. You feel resentment because you can't verbally express what you need to say. You want clarity and closure, but it never comes. You have to ride this ride with bravery. Putting on a brave face and handling the conflicting emotions you experience takes self-control. When you can take a step back to review your emotions with an outside view you actually turn the emotion from a negative to a positive.

Shock

You may walk around like a robot in a constant state of confusion wondering, "What the hell just happened!" Last week you might have been the happiest person in the world never questioning the future of your relationship. Now you feel like you've been hit by an 18-Wheeler and survived with no broken bones. It may be difficult to talk. I mean literally getting words to come out of your mouth takes effort because it hurts to speak.

People believe they're having a conversation with you, when in reality you're nodding your head pretending to comprehend the conversation. You can barely remember their last name.

You now understand the expression "eating like a bird" because you can barely get down a piece of toast. Your appetite is gone. All you want to do is sleep, but you can't. Once you finally dose off, you wake up in the middle of the night with tears in your eyes. The first question you ask yourself is, *"is this real?"*

When a breakup occurs unexpectedly it may seem like it's too much to handle. It could last days or even weeks. You'll want to stay in contact with Mr. Ex to avoid facing the reality that life as you knew it, is about to change. *This is the last thing you need to do at this point even though you feel it would provide the most comfort.* It only prolongs the time it takes you to heal. Face the feelings associated with a breakup head on and move forward.

Denial

You're probably questioning your sanity right now, because nothing you have known to be real is. You thought you were in a relationship meant to last. This is the time where controlling your actions and emotions are crucial. Without exercising control you're going to lose the battle of the breakup. You may want to withdraw from friends and family to avoid talking or even acknowledging the breakup.

Realize that everyone has experienced a breakup and will understand what you're going through. What will separate you from so many women is the way you handle it publicly. The best approach when acquaintances ask about it is by simply replying, "It was great while it lasted, but it was simply time to go our separate ways." And they'll respect you for not boring them with insignificant details they could care less about. *Save your venting for close trusted friends only.*

Anger

Chances are you have gone over and over in your mind a hundred times analyzing what exactly went wrong. There were probably red flags waiving like torches of red-hot fire you ignored. Maybe Mr. Ex *never* introduced you to his friends or his family. Did he stop making plans in advance? Did he disappear for weeks at a time only to reappear? Did he start working out? Did he begin to keep long hours at work? Maybe he acted indifferent towards you when you were around each other.

These are huge warning signs he had something, or someone else going on. Now you're not only mad at him, but you're pissed off at yourself for missing those signs. Maybe you ignored them because you believed it was a phase he was going through. It's perfectly normal to feel anger at this point.

CHAPTER FOUR

WHAT A MAN EXPECTS AFTER A BREAKUP

When a man breaks up with you he expects one thing, and one thing only...You to fall to pieces. He's waiting and anticipating for you to cry, beg him to change his mind, act irrational and create humiliating scenes. He'll be secretly waiting for you to call or text him during middle of the night sobbing, begging, pleading and professing you can't possible live life without him.

STEAL HIS THUNDER

On the other hand when you remain calm, cool and collected it unnerves him. When you drop out of sight he immediately begins asking himself, "Where is she?" He wants to know you miss him and more importantly to provide that extra boost to his fragile ego...*that you need him*. Regardless if he broke up with you or not, it begins to occur to him you may not have been as interested as he initially thought. That's when you'll be back on his radar.

Think of it like the game "Hide-and-go-seek." One player hides, while the other player seeks. If a prolonged amount of time passes with the hider under the impression the seeker has stopped looking, the hider eventually comes out of hiding and actually begins to look for the seeker.

It takes a man at least three weeks to realize you're not actively seeking him out. After four weeks, he's wondering what the hell you're doing. After five to six weeks, chances are he'll be acting like a high school girl wondering where the hell you are, and what the hell you're doing...*if* he cared for you at all. If he hasn't contacted you within eight weeks he's definitely moved on and you should do the same. Don't give him another thought. Don't let it consume your mind. Move on and be marvelous.

BREAKUP POWER PLAY

Mr. Ex has a vision of you in his mind sitting at home on your sofa, crying into a pillow, surrounded by damp crumpled tissues, drowning your sorrows in a pint size of Bluebell Rocky Road. It makes his ego grow one size larger knowing you are suffering. So, when he sees or hears of you out with your best friends actually having fun without him, that you're not even affected by the breakup, it's like quick jab to his pride.

HOW HE BROKE UP AND WHAT IT SAYS ABOUT HIM

Matt LeBlanc once said, "Why do you have to break up with her? Be a man. Just stop calling." But how a man severs his ties is very important and very telling about his character. And remember how a man treats you when no one is watching is the best test you can give a man.

Face to Face

This is a real man with character. In today's high-tech world he's a rare man among men. *He was man enough to tell you in person.* He respected you enough to end the relationship by giving you closure in the best way he could. You won't appreciate a gem like this for a while, but in the end you'll respect this man for having the courage to sit down with you face to face and breaking up with you in a decent manner. A man like this should be admired in today's society where men reduce themselves to boys by breaking up by means of text or email.

Telephone

This is only acceptable in a long distance relationship. Otherwise, it shows he can't handle seeing the look on your face. Not having to face you gives him the courage to breakup.

Email or Text

This is immature, heartless and cold. (*A few other choice words come to mind.*) It says he is a coward and can't face you. He can't even handle a difficult conversation. In short, he doesn't care. Count your blessings this one got away. Don't walk, but run as far away from him as you can.

The Man Who Disappears

The Houdini that disappeared without a trace takes the path of least resistance. He doesn't feel the need to explain himself. There are plenty of men that will leave you dangling just to keep you available as an option for another day. If you've just gone out on a few dates, that's one thing. You don't have a relationship. However, if you've been dating exclusively for three to six months or longer it means he didn't have the spine to tell you you're just not the one for him. Men can't handle tears... it's too much for him. He's not capable of having a hard conversation. He doesn't have a good excuse, so don't waste your time waiting for a bad one. He could care less about your feelings. You're probably someone he's been doing on the side. Trust me this guy isn't worthy to be the water under your feet. Don't give him a second thought. Have another date scheduled before the sun sets tonight.

Men who come and go, in and out of your life are only leaving their options open for another day. He only wants you when it's convenient for him. Let him do it once, fine. Let him do it twice and you can expect a third, fourth and fifth time. If he simply never called you or text you again, leaving you in a state of confusion and bewilderment, have confidence in yourself that you can do better and deserve better. Quit accommodating disrespectful and bad behavior. When you expect more for yourself, guess what? *You get more.*

Do not waste any more of your precious time seeking closure because he has already provided it to you. Oh, I know you feel you need a verbal conversation to obtain closure, but the fact is, a man left you without speaking a word. Leaving you confused, with no clue of any kind, speaks volumes about his character. It reflects he has none. This alone should provide you with all of the closure you need. What the two of you had together didn't even warrant a quick goodbye.

A man who treats your life like a revolving door is just stringing you along. If a man has you ready and willing to do whatever he wants to do, do you really believe he's going to go a week, two weeks, a month or more without sex? Of course he's not. He has you on a rotation. Don't allow him to put you in relationship limbo. Move on to a better man that will adore you, spoil you and provide you with the emotional and physical support you want and deserve. Don't text him. Don't call him. Forget him. Change his name to Mr. Ex.

The Cheater

Kim Cattrall once said, "Men cheat for the same reason that dogs lick their balls...because they can." And let's face it... that's just the simple truth. And because it's easy. Not that I'm justifying it for them. Not that I agree with it and not that it's all right to do, but men cheat because *they can*. And because there is an endless supply of women who have no standards, or requirements and who are more than willing to accommodate them.

I've heard people say "forgive and forget." Well, if you cannot forget, how can you ever forgive? If you are struggling with the decision to stick around or cut him loose, ask yourself what kind of affair it was and how you found out? Was it a one-time slip up that he was so riddled with guilt over that he confessed his sin? Were you tipped off by a third-party? Or, was it full-fledged affair that took place over months or even years? Did you have to turn into a female version of Sherlock Holmes to figure out what the hell was going on? Was there premeditated sex? Vacations? Did he take her on business trips to entertain clients, spend time with her family and have preplanned rendezvous?

The one time affair is the easiest to forgive. Again I'm not implying that it's okay, but women will come closer to forgiving this type of affair. Men are weak. He made a mistake. If it was the second kind you need to know this... That's not called an affair, *that's called a double life* and it's the ultimate slap in the face to you as a woman. So, if you're asking yourself if you should forgive this type of affair, maybe a better question to ask yourself is "Why in the hell would you?"

This kind of man is a master manipulator who let you believe a lie (that he was committed to you, that he loved you) for months, years or maybe longer. He let the other woman believe the same. Even if the old saying is true, "all men cheat" perhaps you would be better off finding a man that is smart enough, not to get caught.

Do not blame yourself, don't take responsibility for his actions and don't think there was something you were doing wrong. The problem lies within him. A relationship consists of two people, not three. When a third person is invited, where only two people belong, it is an uneven playing field. Don't let it humiliate you, hurt you, or fill your head with insecurities. If there was a problem he should have come to you long before going to another woman. And nine times out of ten a man cheats with someone that's not half as good as what he had at home. So shift it in reverse, sit back and let him have her...she's not near the woman you are. Don't demean yourself by competing and don't be jealous...you know what she's getting - *a man that's unfaithful, a liar and a cheat.* Sleep soundly knowing that she's sleeping next to that every night.

Steve Harvey said it best in his book *Act Like a Lady, Think Like a Man: What Men Really Think About Love, Relationships, Intimacy, and Commitment,* when he said, "Women can go over it again and again in their minds, finding all kinds of deficiencies in themselves-"I didn't do this right," "I wasn't good enough," "I didn't love him the way I should," "she came in here and outperformed me"-but the fact still remains that he didn't have any business cheating. So women need to release themselves from the blame of a cheating man's actions-just do that for yourselves. Because holding on to that baggage can be paralyzing; it can cripple you and keep you from performing in your next encounter. You simply cannot drive forward if you're focused on what's happening in the rearview mirror."

GIVE YOUR HEART TIME TO CATCH UP WITH YOUR BRAIN

If you're still struggling with the decision to stay or go after discovering an affair, realize you may still be in love with him simply because your heart hasn't had time to catch up with your brain. *No contact* is exactly what you need to think with a clear mind. Soon those feelings of love may turn into feelings of nausea when you think of how disrespectful this man has treated you. Cut him loose and don't look back.

WHY YOU CAN'T BE 'JUST FRIENDS'

Sarah Dessen best described why you can't remain friends in her book *This Lullaby* when she wrote, "Because you can never go from going out to being friends, just like that. It's a lie. It's just something that people say they'll do to take the permanence out of a breakup. And someone always takes it to mean more than it does, and then is hurt even more when, inevitably, said 'friendly' relationship is still a major step down from the previous relationship, and it's like breaking up all over again. But messier."

What do you do when a man breaks up, and delivers the "Let's be friends" line? You smile and say, "Sure we can." The next time he calls, or texts...choose the option to ignore him. When he asks you out to dinner, a simple "no thanks" will do.

There is a reason behind the "we can be friends" line when delivered during a breakup that only feeds his ego. It makes him feel like less of an ass than he is. He feels guilty for breaking up, and believes by offering his friendship he is being a great guy. It's an easy out. Don't blow up when he suggests this. Smile, say "Of course we can," excuse yourself and make your exit appear so effortlessly, it makes his head spin. Leave the premises. Disappear from his radar.

Another reason Mr. Ex is asking you to be "just friends" is because he is uncertain if really wants to let you go permanently. He's unsure if you are worth keeping around and wants to explore his options. By asking you to be "just friends" he wants to keep you available as backup in case the other woman, or women on his 'to do' list fail to work out. Forget him and find a man who wants to be your best friend and lover. In a very "friendly" way, move past Mr. Ex quickly.

Courage is the most important of all the virtues, because without courage you can't practice any other virtue consistently. You can practice any virtue erratically, but nothing consistently without courage.

MAYA ANGELOU

CHAPTER FIVE

CUT HIM OFF COMPLETELY

When you are in an intimate, sexual relationship with a man you become bonded by oxytocin, a hormone that flows through your veins like a tsunami. It takes over your emotions and you become addicted to that man. You bond with him. That's why you see many women completely lose their minds after a breakup. Because they believe they'll never find another man like Mr. Ex, when in fact, it's the hormone oxytocin. Don't fool yourself and give into the notion that Mr. Ex is the only man for you. Understand any man with a pulse and a penis can provide it. Which is why you'd better be very selective with who you have sex with.

AFTER A BREAKUP, DON'T MAKE THE MISTAKE OF HAVING SEX WITH MR. EX UNTIL HIS ACTIONS PROVE HIS LOVE FOR YOU

No matter how hard you were to get in the beginning of a relationship, never be easy to get after a breakup. It will only lead to him becoming bored once again and will eventually take you for granted. Or worse, he'll view you as a plaything. Men marry women they adore, cherish and the key element that sends a man out to buy the ring: *Respect*. You'll never win him over by being easily seduced, or the girl that drops everything to be with him. And if he doesn't respect you as woman you should just cut your losses now.

Understand that just because Mr. Ex wants to sleep with you does not mean he loves you or is even thinking about a future with you. And it definitely does not mean that he is seeking a reconciliation with you.

WHEN A MAN LOVES A WOMAN

He'll put your feelings above his own. He'll care about you, your family and anything else you consider important. He'll be happy for you when something exciting happens in your life. And will never want to cause you one minute of pain. *It would actually cause him pain to see you hurt.* You'll know without question a man values you, because you'll feel it with every ounce of your being. You won't need to hear his profession of love, because his actions prove it.

You'll never question if he's thinking of you during the day because he constantly communicates by emails, texts messages, phone calls, lunch dates and is making future plans to see you. You'll never question if he has your best interests at heart because you'll never doubt what his motives are.

Steve Harvey described it best in his book *Act Like a Lady, Think Like a Man* when he explained the mindset of a man when it comes to loving the woman he is committed to. The three "P's" that make up the DNA of a man. Profess. Provide. Protect. When a man loves you, he'll profess his love. Meaning he will always introduce you as his lady, girlfriend, wife or significant other. A man will always protect you to make sure that no harm will come your way emotionally or physically. Last but not least, a man that loves and cares for you will provide for you in whatever capacity he can.

NO MAN'S AFRAID OF A LITTLE CONFLICT

Arguments and disagreements not only test a relationship, but also show you how strong one is. If he's not willing to have a hard conversation with you to work out conflicts then cut him off and move on. You want a man that is a rock of strength, not one that vanishes at the first sign of trouble. Relationships take two people willing to occasionally set their pride aside and admit when they're wrong, or that they have made a mistake.

If a man breaks up with you for any reason, or disappears for a week or longer you need to really step back and look at the relationship for what it is. This means if he tells you he needs time to think about what he wants, or the worst... when he just falls off the face of the earth without giving an explanation...**you need to cut him off and disappear!** To take you seriously he has to put you in a different category than he does the other women on his rotation. And in order for him to view you differently he has to know without doubt you'll kick him to curb at the first sign of disrespect.

(Now, I'm not talking about the guy you went out with a few times and he never called you again. I'm talking about the man you had a real relationship with. The man you believed you would spend the rest of your life with.)

For example, let's say a man told you he needed time to sort out his feelings. Turn the tables on him so to speak. When he resurfaces let it be a few weeks before he can find you. Men know they are supposed to place a phone call!

If you've been intimate with him and he goes silent, the smart girl does not give him a second chance. There is simply no excuse for it. These men know they are screwing up. Make it clear to him you expect a man to be present in your life. If he can't handle that, don't only show him the door, open it wide enough so he can easily walk through it. And guess what, you'll earn his admiration for doing this and at the same time, protect your heart. It's a win, win.

Let him know from the beginning he walked out on the relationship and you have no time for a man that treats your life like a revolving door. When you put your foot down you'll earn his respect. And when you earn a man's respect, you'll have him right where he belongs...wrapped around your little finger.

Always remember that 'a monkey knows what trees he can climb'. When you **ignore** a man's blatant disrespect it only guarantees it will continue. You need not tell him that he has to work for you, but don't make it easy for him. Continue to move forward with your life without skipping a beat.

Men only appreciate what they have to work hard for. You may have found yourself being too available and accommodating. You may think it is what a man wants, but in truth they want a challenge. *Men crave a challenge.*

More important than good looks, a great body or the size of his bank account is how well a man treats you. The best way to know it's all right to give your heart to a man is to put him through a little testing. And this takes place over time and before you sleep with him. If he's not passing your tests, know in advance in your mind you have to keep your options open, and throw this one in the dating pool. (See Chapter Ten.)

Take notice of how a man treats you, cares for you and how he protects you. I'm not necessarily talking about protecting you from attackers invading your home or city. *(Although should that happen he'd better be right by your side.)* Does he check to make sure the air in your tires are full before going on an out-of-town trip? Does he make sure you're not being taken advantage of when you buy a car? Does he make sure you have everything you need, to do whatever you have to do that particular day? Does he remember birthdays, holidays and plan a romantic dinner for Valentines? Does he listen? Does he do what he says he's going to do? Does he call when he says he's going to call? Does he care about your safety during bad weather? Is he proud of you? Does he want to show you off? Does he introduce you to his friends and family? Does he do little things to make you happy? And most importantly does he protect your heart? A man that cares for you would never do you harm emotionally.

If your answer is no to most of these questions you should ask yourself why you are allowing this man to remain in your life? What's the benefit of dating a man that isn't enhancing your already great life?

When you find a man who treats you well this is the man you should appreciate and should be the grand prize winner of your heart. Not the man that causes tears to flow from your eyes.

Before you offer your heart again make sure he is passing your tests. Make sure his actions are proving his love to you... not just his words.

KNOW WHEN TO CUT THE STRINGS

- Don't settle for an on again off again relationship. It's unhealthy and will only make your happiness feel like a roller coaster ride with highs, lows, ups and downs. You deserve better!

- Just like small children men will test you to see what they can get away with. Standing your ground, holding on to your own beliefs, convictions and knowing when your kindness is being taken for granted will earn his respect.

- You must constantly evaluate your relationship and ask yourself if you're getting what you want and need out of it. Identify your needs. Do you need more affection? Attention? Security? Companionship? More sex? If you're not getting what you need you won't be happy. If you've nicely told him what your needs are and he doesn't step up to meet them, know that it's time to move on. Don't settle for a man that isn't meeting all of your needs.

IS HE STRINGING YOU ALONG?

There are men that simply do not know what they want. If this is the case, know you are not in his life to fix any unresolved issues he may have. Let another woman waste her precious time.

If he is stringing you along, don't fool yourself by believing you can change him. Only he can make the necessary changes in his life. When you decide to completely cut him off he'll either decide to make those changes or he won't. If he doesn't step up for you, accept the fact that you have dodged a bullet and be thankful you didn't allow him to waste anymore of your precious time.

Some men simply don't deserve a second chance and you may have given him twenty. Know you deserve the best a man has to offer and refuse to settle for crumbs. If Mr. Ex is keeping you on the fence, now would be the perfect time to tell him you hope he calls when he figures out what he wants out of life. In the mean time you will not be waiting for him. Your next move is to let your actions speak louder than any words you could ever communicate and go completely silent. Adopt this old saying and repeat it to yourself every day, *"Men are like trains, one comes by every five minutes."*

You must understand you will never be able to move on in love if you continue to stay in touch with Mr. Ex. Only when you emotionally detach yourself will you be available, open and ready for love with Mr. Right. And Mr. Right is the man who will meet your physical and emotional needs without fail and without you having to ask for it. Just because your relationship status changed overnight doesn't mean your basic needs do. The sooner you begin the *No Contact* rule, you enable yourself to emotionally heal from the inside, which will free you to be emotionally available for Mr. Right.

If you keep Mr. Ex around, you will only remain in love with him and it is only natural to want something you can't have. If you keep him in your life he may continue to hurt you. Be smart enough to recognize when two people have different needs and mature enough to realize it will never work out and just let go. The more you stay in contact with him the longer it will be before you can actually move on. Feelings defy logic... know your mind well enough to know when you're not thinking logically. When you're thinking with your heart and not your mind you don't make solid, clear choices.

Jackie Mason said, "Eighty percent of married men cheat in America. The rest cheat in Europe." And chances are Mr. Ex lives in America. He may just be selfish and want his cake in one hand, ice cream in the other and you sitting there feeding it to him with a silver spoon. Do not under any circumstances compete for his love with another woman. When you compete you demean yourself. And it sends a loud and clear message of desperation. He may have two women who provide him with and fulfill different needs of his own. Regardless of how well the two of you meshed, accept the fact you'll never be able to make him happy. Move on to someone who will make his mission in life to keep you happy and satisfied. Love yourself enough to move on. Keep him on the *ex-list* forever.

INTUITION...A GIRLS BEST FRIEND

That indescribable feeling you get that says "Something is not quite right here." It's been referred to as a whisper from God. Listen to it, trust it and let it be your best friend. Kim Basinger said "I feel there are two people inside me - me and my intuition. If I go against her, she'll screw me every time, and if I follow her, we get along quite nicely.

There is nothing stronger or more powerful than a woman's intuition. Unfortunately, many women confuse intuition with insecurities. Especially when it comes to matters of the heart. This is the time when you need to trust your intuition the most. If you believe you're being insecure, maybe a good question to ask yourself is "What am I being insecure about?" Your intuition will tell you something is wrong, but it's your job to determine what it is. Whether a man is lying, cheating or maybe you just feel he doesn't have your best interests at heart. Whatever the case may be find the underlying cause of it.

It's inevitable that loneliness will ultimately follow immediately after a breakup. It could be you're allowing him to fill the void you feel if you continue to communicate with him. You'll never be able to move on completely to Mr. Right if you're in a constant state of limbo.

Not knowing where you stand in a relationship is like walking on glass... You'll always be afraid of breaking it. *And by the way,* if you have to ask where you stand in a relationship that is a big, flashing neon warning sign that there is *no relationship*! If a man loves you, you'll never question where his heart is. He will never place doubt in your mind. You'll actually feel the love he has for you, not because he has told you, but because his actions show and prove it every single day.

Know that remaining in touch after a breakup will cause you to feel loyal to him. This is a hard one for some women to get past. Please don't make the mistake of refusing dates because you still feel as if you belong to a man that has chosen not to be in your life. Wake up! Do not think for five minutes Mr. Ex is home feeling sorry for himself on a Saturday night. Chances are after the breakup he was scrolling through his contact list looking for your replacement before God got the news. Start making yourself available to Mr. Right and unavailable to Mr. Ex.

During your relationship you probably took yourself off the market and made yourself unavailable to all the eligible men that were pursuing you. If you allow Mr. Ex to remain in your life you may not give those eligible bachelors that deserve a date with you a chance.

Make your mind up that you are not going to let a breakup, break you. You can allow it to be as messy as you want or handle it with class. By starting with *No Contact*, it gives you both the time and space you need to gather your thoughts and think with a clear head. Gain control of your emotions so that eventually you both can speak calmly in a mature way to one another.

You have to take some time to regain your composure. *No Contact* is the very best way to emotionally and physically detach from Mr. Ex. Cut the ties that bind and heal your heart. You can't heal if you're constantly waiting around for the old relationship to fix itself. You'll never be able to move on to bigger, better love. Accept that if it is meant to be, it will be. But for the time being you are not going to wait around for love to come knocking on your door. Sometimes you have to get out and invite love in.

*I think of life itself now as a wonderful play that I've
written for myself, and so my purpose is to have the utmost fun
playing my part.*

SHIRLEY MacLAINE

CHAPTER SIX

HIDE YOUR CRAZY

There are a few news headlines that have caught my attention over the years. The one I will never forget is that of Lisa Nowak, the former NASA astronaut. She won't be remembered as a famous, kick ass female astronaut, but rather as the woman who drove over 900 miles, wearing an adult diaper so that she would not be inconvenienced with bathroom breaks in route to kidnap her ex-boyfriends, new girlfriend. *What the hell?* I wonder, do you think she expected a reconciliation after that?

If you are plotting revenge in any way, shape or form stop right now in your tracks. It's time to face the cold, hard truth of reality. **Forever does not really mean...** *forever*. Relationships start and end every day. And when one door closes, it's true that another opens.

The only time you will truly ever be satisfied and obtain closure with a breakup is when you are the one breaking up. Accept the fact unless a breakup ends on your terms any breakup you experience in the future will end with pain and heartache.

I've seen women as dignified as Grace Kelly lose their ever-loving minds when it comes to men. You know the girl that won't let go, or go away. I bet you have at least one girlfriend who mentally lost it after a breakup. Maybe you were that girl. We've all had our pathetic moments.

I want to start with what lengths the most sensible women will go to after the initial stages of a breakup to gain attention. If you catch yourself doing anything out of the ordinary lean to family and friends and seek help during this time.

You may have heard the old expression "Idle hands are the devils workshop." The same is true if think and obsess over Mr. Ex. Keep your mind and body busy to avoid allowing emotions to override your logic and do anything drastic. Think about the future. What do you think Mr. Ex will have to say about you while enjoying dinner with his friends or family? Will you be the crazy girl that wouldn't go away? Or, will you be the one he regrets losing?

So let us take a look at some of the drastic measures women will take to get attention after a breakup. Shall we? Make a promise to yourself you will not be *"that girl."*

- **Sending endless text messages.** You want Mr. Ex to know how you feel and to understand how much pain you're experiencing. You want him to know without a doubt you love him and how much you're hurting. You believe by conveying this information to him, he'll come back to you. ***You're wrong!*** *The only* message you're sending to Mr. Ex is you are going a little crazy. And he's eating it up. He's looking at his phone blowing up and thinking, "I can't believe she's falling apart like this." Again, you're feeding his super-size ego. It's a fact men and women are usually within three feet of their cell phone. *He received your message!* A good rule to live by is if you send a text message and receive no response--you should never send a second one. Ask yourself this question "What good would a text do anyway?" Real relationships require face-to-face conversations during conflict, not text messages. Conversations through text messages are for teenagers.

- **The Accidental Text.** He knows the accidental text ploy. No *"accidentally"* sending a text message to him by mistake to later claim it was intended for your sisters-cousins, best friends-brother. No nothing. Silence.

- **Calling repeatedly.** If you dial his number know in advance Mr. Ex is going to hit the option to ignore your call. If he does answer chances are you'll let your emotions take over and trust me, nothing good or productive will come from a heated exchange. When you're under a great deal of emotional stress the more likely you are to say words you really don't mean and will ultimately regret. Besides, Mr. Ex will have nothing to say that can or will bring you the closure you need. If he ignores your call, it's just going to rip your heart out all over again. No calling by mistake, delete his number, block his number if you must or sit on your hands, read a book, go for a jog, or email me! ***Do anything but dial his number!***

- **Begging/pleading with Mr. Ex to take you back.** Would you date a man who cried, begged and pleaded for you to date him? *No, I didn't think so.* It would make him appear desperate and pathetic, right? Desperate and pathetic is the exact image you're portraying to him if you call, text or show up at his house without an invitation in a drunken stupor sobbing *"I can't live without you."* Have some pride and know the value you bring to a relationship. Again, think long term, not short term satisfaction. You want to be the woman of his dreams and I can assure you the woman of his dreams isn't a woman who is a complete mess.

- **Blocking your number, calling and hanging up.** Mr. Ex knows it's you calling. Stop it! No attempts to contact him whatsoever. It's creepy and falls under harassment.

- **Driving by his house.** Unless you live next door there's really no excuse for driving by his home. It falls under stalker/harassing behavior. Most men and women consider this a major turn off (and illegal).

- **Frequenting places you know he'll be.** If you work together there's really nothing you can do, but try to avoid him at all costs. If you frequented the same places find another place to frequent. Right now you need to be scarce. If you have children together the same applies. Deal with the issues at hand in a calm, mature manner and find your exit as quickly as possible.

- **Sending emails.** No desperately seeking closure emails. No "Hi, how are you?" No wishing him a Merry Christmas, Happy New Year or Happy Birthday. Not a peep!

- **Letting him know you're falling apart.** A man doesn't take a woman back because she confessed she couldn't live without him. This cries out "desperation" and you won't be an exception. Have some pride and know that what is attractive to a man is a woman who is independent and self-sufficient.

- **Cursing, telling him he'll never find anyone better.** First, *it's just not pretty* and if you do this he'll make a point to find someone better. And you're only showing your ass. Again, think long term. Think back to what made him fall in love with you to begin with and be *that woman*.

- **Cyber Stalking.** This is a tough one that requires massive self-control. Why? Because it's right there...

at your manicured fingertips! What your ex does from this point on is none of your concern. Ask yourself if you really want to know what new girls appear as his friends or followers. This will only hurt you in the end and make you a little crazy along the way. Block him. Delete him. Do whatever you have to do, but do yourself a favor and refrain from becoming obsessed with his social networking activity.

- **Dealing with friends and family.** If you had the same friends by all means remain friends, just remember they are his friends also. When you run in to them make small talk and be on your way. No bashing Mr. Ex. Don't even mention his name. Only if they bring him up in conversation should you reply with something complimentary about him. No tears or breakdowns. Do nothing that would give the impression you're allowing this breakup to bring you down. Put on a performance that would make Glenn Close green with envy.

- **Attempting to make Mr. Ex jealous.** Mr. Ex will see any attempts to make him jealous as the desperate-attention-seeking methods they truly are. Right now is not the time for this type of behavior and he won't find it attractive. Don't go out to rub it in his face. Rather, go out to enjoy yourself and to move on.

Don't *act* as if you have a full life, actually *have* a full life.

- **Don't look desperate on Social Media Sites.** Look at what you posted in the previous two months prior to the breakup. That's what you should continue to post. Nothing out of the ordinary that makes you appear as if you're grasping for attention. Post what you normally post and avoid pictures of you out partying until four o'clock in the morning. The same applies to posting sad, depressing expressions of love. Your friends don't want to get depressed on a social networking site. Don't check-in to every nightclub. Continue to be the beautiful, respectful, fun woman he fell in love with. Any attempts to get his attention during this time will only backfire and make you look a mess.

- **No ex sex.** If sex was what tied relationships together everyone would be blissfully married. Sex didn't prevent him from breaking up with you, sex didn't keep him by your side and sex is not going to make him come back to you now. I don't care how sad he sounds or how much he tells you he misses you. No sex before monogamy. If he just broke up with you it's safe to assume you're no longer in a monogamous relationship. To have sex with you again, he will need to prove his love for you.

Imagine how constantly calling, sending text messages or accidentally running into him will make you look. It will mortify him and he will mentally file your pretty face in the 'crazy' category.

You may also believe a friendly harmless text message to Mr. Ex, just to remind him you are still out in the world, will do no harm and will actually remind him of all the warm fuzzy feelings the two of you once shared. Let me assure you that Mr. Ex knows where you are and how to find you. There is no need to send a reminder. Besides, if he needs a reminder to call you, do you really want him anyway?

Understand there is really nothing that could possibly keep a man away from a woman he loves. He has the same means of communication you have. He still has your number. Please do not fool yourself to believe sending a pointless text message will magically make change his mind and come running in your direction.

You may very well be pursing Mr. Ex after the breakup and not even realize it. You may be seeking closure in an attempt to save the broken relationship. It's very likely towards the end of the relationship, Mr. Ex began to detach himself emotionally. Chances are he stopped initiating calls, texts and stopped making plans in advance. When this happened you may have unintentionally shifted into the pursuer mode without even knowing that you were doing it. It is very possible you started chasing him when he stopped providing you with the attention you needed. Some of the signs that you may have been pursing him include, but are not limited, to calling him, texting, emailing, making arrangements for a date night or just to see him. In our modern society we often forget it is a man's job to do everything in his power to make us happy. Not the other way around. When a man loves you, he is going to want to see you. You will not have to remind him to call, plan lunch or dinner dates because he'll be one step ahead of the game.

The list could go on and on. Understand every single action you take will be viewed as a sign of desperation and neediness and is massaging his ego. And the second you start compromising for the sake of massaging a man's ego, that's it, game over.

Your only job is to show him you can live without him. Show him you do not need him and you might be surprised how fast he comes looking for you. Most importantly -- ***make your exit with class, dignity and pride intact.***

―――――――――

I've never loved another person the way I love myself.

MAE WEST

―――――――――

CHAPTER SEVEN

HANDLING A BREAKUP THROUGH FACEBOOK AND TWITTER

Winona Ryder once said, "Breakups are hard for anybody, but it's particularly tough when it's being documented and you see the person's picture everywhere. Most people don't have that added problem when they breakup with someone." And if that's true Facebook and Twitter have leveled the playing field.

You've probably done what every head over heels girl in love has done and posted sweet picture after picture of you and Mr. Ex looking blissful and beautiful. The two of you appeared to be the "it" couple. Your friends never saw you happier. Now the shame and embarrassment of another failed relationship rears its ugly head.

For the sake of argument I am going to assume you are not happy about the breakup. How do you handle it on Facebook and Twitter?

The main question after a breakup is:

"Do I delete him from my friends list?"

The answer --**Yes, you delete him**. The reason *why* is simple. For a man to want you, he has to miss you. He cannot possibly experience what life is like without you if he sees your pretty face in a post or tweet every day. Nor will he feel the need to call if all he has to do is logon on to the nearest computer to find out what you're doing, how you're feeling and where you're going. You're taking away any incentive he has to actually pick up the phone and find out.

The second question is:

"How do I face my six hundred and fifty-eight friends and followers right in the middle of a breakup?"

Look at it this way... You and Mr. Ex are the only two people on God's green earth that currently know you are going through a breakup. (Along with a few friends you are depending on for the emotional support you need.) The smart girl quietly takes down any photographs (especially profile pictures that include Mr. Ex). Or she moves them to an album where privacy settings are set to private. Don't remain in a fantasy relationship that no longer exists. Delete and move forward.

Making a public announcement is not required or necessary. Just as you phased him in your life, phase him out. When friends and family bring up the subject, with a smile simply reply, "Sometimes things just don't work out." Everyone has endured a breakup and will understand. And the respect you will earn when you take the high road and refrain from bashing Mr. Ex is immeasurable.

Look at what you have posted in the past. Do you post pictures of great food, your kids or check into favorite restaurants you frequent? Continue to make posts in the same manner you have done in the past few weeks or months. If you never posted anything before, no need to start now.

If you begin to post or tweet every aspect of your life to prove to the world how happy you are, it will only draw attention. People see right through this charade. The same is true if you start posting or tweeting veiled innuendos directed at Mr. Ex. It's very tempting to go on a posting rampage to express your feelings, but ultimately will make your friends uncomfortable and want to avoid you completely.

Don't bad mouth Mr. Ex to your six-hundred and fifty-eight friends. Just because he's not the "Knight in Shining Armor" you once believed him to be doesn't mean your friends share your opinion. If you dated for a good amount of time you both probably have mutual friends in common. Word will get back to him that you've either smeared his name or that you spoke complimentary words. If you choose the first option it only confirms in his mind the split was in his best interest.

If you had your relationship status set to "In a Relationship" your first impulse will be to change it to "Single." Don't be so quick. Rather, wait at least three days and change it privately. Preset your settings to private, in advance, to avoid posting it on your newsfeed.

If you want to grab Mr. Ex's attention go completely silent for two weeks. Gradually start posting pictures of yourself with friends looking fabulous. Don't overdo it. Just enough to let him know you are not an emotional wreck and can carry on just fine without him. Word will get back to him through your mutual friends.

I hear of some women deleting their Facebook and/or Twitter accounts after a breakup. *Excuse me…*Are you trying to tell the world, specifically Mr. Ex that you are handling a breakup like a two old? It gives the impression you are sad, lonely and pathetic. It sends the message you cannot even handle a breakup. And remember, in the grand overall design a breakup is…***just a breakup.*** It's the end of one chapter before another begins.

Take an attitude that a breakup is not a breakdown. You have no choice but to move on and be even more amazing than before. Deleting your social media account sends the message you are having a hard time. If you do anything, choose, not to logon for a while. Remember, the world will only know what you put out for everyone to see.

At the end of the day, what proves you are a class act is when you can remain calm, cool and collected even in times of trouble.

I've been through it all baby, I'm mother courage.

ELIZABETH TAYLOR

CHAPTER EIGHT

HOW LONG WILL I HAVE TO GO WITHOUT CONTACT?

When you ask yourself how long you should wait before contacting Mr. Ex, **one of the best rules to live by is this**...Don't contact a man to begin with. *Why*? Because it's a form of pursuing him and a man runs from anything that chases him. Look, I'm not crazy about this rule either. Had I been a part of the decision-making process when our great, great, grandmothers, mother came up with the "Women don't call men," rule I would have objected. *Demanded they reconsider*. But, we all know it's time and tested good advice. We've known since the beginning of time men like to be hunters... Let him hunt you. And *learn to enjoy being hunted*. If you're the one that contacts him, how will you ever know he sincerely *wants* you? Make a vow to yourself that you won't chase a man even if he grabs your purse and runs with it.

You may try to justify to yourself that it is perfectly fine to call him now because you have been in a long-term relationship and the rules don't apply to you. This unfortunately is where many women go wrong. **Now, more than ever you have to sit back and let him initiate contact first.**

Calling Mr. Ex sends the message you are clingy and desperate. For a man to want anything, you have to make him think it was *his* idea. To make him think it's his idea you have to get him to lower his guard, otherwise he'll run in the opposite direction.

If you do break down and call him, he might be polite and reply. You may ask if he's available for lunch or dinner. And he may even be polite and accept your invitation only because the other girl he is seeing is busy that day.

Learn a lesson from Hanna who sent a little text message to John the man who broke up with her unexpectedly. Three weeks after the breakup she was still devastated. Against her better judgment she sent him a text message just to say she was thinking of him. John responded, which thrilled Hanna. Another three days went by and he sent her another text. Hanna was elated John was showing signs of interest again. Things progressed and they saw each other the following weekend and he continued to call and acted as if nothing ever happened. She believed he just needed space. That is until the other woman, he had begun to date that lived out of town, had a free weekend without her kids. John was using two women to keep his time occupied.

I've taken a brutally honest excerpt from Greg Behrendt and Amiira Ruotola Behrendts book *It's Called a Breakup, Because It's Broken,* which sums it up pretty accurately as to why a man's not calling. "If he's not calling you, it's because you are not on his mind. If he creates expectations for you, and then doesn't follow through on little things, he will do same for big things. Be aware of this and realize that he's okay with disappointing you. Don't be with someone who doesn't do what they say they're going to do. If he's choosing not to make a simple effort that would put you at ease and bring harmony to a recurring fight, then he doesn't respect your feelings and needs. "Busy" is another word for "asshole." "Asshole" is another word for the guy you're dating. You deserve a fucking phone call."

I may begin to sound like a broken record, but let me emphasize again, men do not need a reminder to call you! Have a sense of pride and self-respect. And know if he's not dialing your number, he's not worthy of your time. Don't subject yourself to being treated poorly and know if you're unhappy in anyway, he simply is not treating you the way you deserve. If you are the one making phone calls it sends a message to a man that you're insecure, needy and that you don't have other options. And maybe you don't... but he doesn't have to know this information. Imagine him looking at his phone with a grin that would make the Joker look bashful. He's thinking to himself, "I've got this one on the hook." If he's interested in you, he won't make you feel like an option.

Immediately start working to enhance your own life. Focus on elevating your life to a higher one. By not losing your cool after a breakup, knowing you handled the situation with grace, class and dignity will give your confidence a tremendous boost and more importantly, you demonstrate with your actions that you're a woman with self-control. And when he knows you can handle yourself, it raises your value.

When you choose to start *No Contact*, it may seem you're defeating your purpose if your purpose is to see Mr. Ex again. Women tend to want instant gratification and taking two months of your life to accomplish that seems drastic. Remember it's not about an immediate fix. It's about creating a long-term relationship and taking time to gain the insight and clarity you need to fix a broken relationship, or move past a bad one. When you make your mind up that you can be upbeat regardless of what life throws at you, that's empowerment.

It's only natural for you to want the one person that hurt you to hold you in their arms and give you the reassurance you need that all will be fine. More importantly you want him to stop this foolish behavior and just fix the breakup! It's unfortunate, breakups just don't work like that, but you have to have a clear understanding that if a man isn't contributing his fifty percent to make the relationship work, then you need to make him feel that you are losing interest and drop out of sight.

When you take time to compose yourself after a breakup, you can be assured that if you hold it together, behave in such a way and get your emotions in check you'll be able to communicate with clarity when Mr. Ex does call. On the other hand, after a month or two passes, you may not want anything to do with him... and that's fine too.

If you believe Mr. Ex is Mr. Right and want to get him back I'm rooting for you. I believe in true love. If there is a person that you feel connected with and believe in your heart it's meant to be, who am I, or anyone else to tell you differently.

If you fear not contacting him will make him forget you, you need not worry. Absence truly does make the heart grow fonder. Maybe you want to work out the kinks in your relationship and if you do, you have to change your mindset that you're not going to lift one finger to fix it. Instead sit back, have patience and let the man do the hard work. This isn't easy... it's hard and not for the weak. The weak will fail and learn the hard way only to experience one painful breakup after another.

Realistically, if the two of you really shared a deep connection, Mr. Ex will have made contact with you within thirty days. If Mr. Ex makes No Contact within sixty days it's very safe to assume your relationship is over. By the end of this time frame if you have focused on your own life, you may not even notice. You haven't been wallowing around in self-pity... You've been busy making your life a fabulous one. In the end whether he reaches out to you or not, you've made a clean break and haven't lost your pride in the process.

Know if you decide you want Mr. Ex back, you have to establish and create a new relationship. A relationship that will be better than before because you refuse to accept less than the best. Women have forgotten that they are in control of the relationships they allow in their life. You have what a man wants and don't ever forget it. Don't hand over the reins for him to guide you unless he's providing you with the security and confidence that he's capable of leading you in the right direction.

After all those years as a woman hearing "not thin enough, not pretty enough, not smart enough, not this enough, not that enough,' almost overnight I woke up one morning and thought, 'I'm enough.'

ANNA QUINDLEN

CHAPTER NINE

GET YOUR HOUSE IN ORDER

There is no nice way to say this so, I'll just say it. After you've been through a breakup, it is only normal that your self-confidence feels like it's been bitch slapped to the curb. It does not matter if you are the most beautiful woman in the world with everything to offer, you will still feel as if you've been sucker punched in the gut. You may not feel attractive or pretty. You may ask the universe why you cannot find love. We've all been there. We've all had our ugly day, but now it it imperative you snap out of this dark place, post haste!

How do you move on past a breakup? You constantly tell yourself that there are simply no other options but to move on. You take time to work on yourself, you immediately find social gatherings to attend and reach out to friends and family. Join a spin class. Take up dancing. Find a hobby...*Do something!* When you have revolved your life around a relationship it's easy to fall victim to the daily grind and put your needs on the back burner. And it's hard to put on a brave face and go out when you're facing the gloom of a breakup. But go out you must! Get dolled up and hit the town. A change of scenery does wonders to lift a girl's spirits. Just get busy about being passionate about your life. Do this and men will be beating down your door.

Chances are getting back in the dating world is the last thought on your mind. Often you need to go into dating detox immediately to get your life back on track. Think back to where you were emotionally when you met Mr. Ex. I'll bet you were at place in your life where you were open, ready to give love and ready to receive it. A woman's basic needs are love, attention and affection. As I've said before, those needs don't go away when a relationship ends. You'll eventually want to find someone that is not only capable of lavishing you with affection and attention, but wants to cater to your every need.

Let me ask you this. Do you love yourself? Are you happy with yourself? Really think about that question. If not take some time... two weeks or longer if need be to get right with the person that matters most...*you*. We attract men that mirror ourselves; the law of attraction is that likes attract likes. So if you are not in love with yourself, or even in like with yourself chances are it's going to be hard to attract a man that not only loves you, but likes you too.

During this time forget about dating. Forget about Mr. Ex, finding Mr. Right and understand that there is no man in the world that your happiness should depend on. Sure, one may make you *feel* happy, but let's be clear about this... you have to make yourself happy first. It's great when you do meet someone that enhances or adds value to your life, but you have to be in a place where you can say, "I have a great life and I'm looking for someone to share my great life with and build on that. If that's not what you're looking for, I understand. Call me when you figure it out."

Maybe you don't want to start dating right off the bat. But you can take time to make a few adjustments to enhance your life and keep you occupied at the same time. I know it's not easy to go from unhappy to happy at the flip of a switch, but reflect on what makes you content and fulfilled. It's imperative to always seek out ways to improve your life and to be open to the possibility of love when it comes knocking. That is what's great about *No Contact* … it gives you time to gain perspective in all aspects of your life.

During the first month of *No Contact,* make a list of everything you enjoy doing, but neglected while in a relationship. Do whatever you have to do to make yourself feel beautiful and amazing. Start with the basics:

- **Get a Mini-Makeover** -- Don't do anything drastic, but make a subtle change in your appearance. Maybe you wanted to try out a new hairstyle, or get some highlights. Treat yourself to manicure and a pedicure. A full-blown spa day does wonders to lift a girl's spirits, helps you to relax and makes you look and feel great. Make an appointment to feel great.

- **What Does Your Wardrobe Say About You?** -- You don't have to wear designer labels, but if you've been walking into the bookstore (or anywhere) with sweats and a t-shirt on then stop it! Always do the best with what you have to work with. If you can afford a little shopping spree then make a date with yourself to go shopping. It occupies your time, you'll look forward to it and when you do wear your new clothes the vibe you send out will be that of confidence and happiness. When you look good, you feel good.

- ***When is the last time you've contacted an old friend?*** -- Yes, you remember the ones you neglected when you became busy with Mr. Ex. Go through your contact list and send a text message to at least five of your friends. It could open up a conversation or two and even lead to a lunch date or even better, dinner. Again, it'll make you happy, send out a great vibe and give you a positive mental attitude.

- **Hit the Gym** -- Now more than ever it's important to keep yourself healthy. It'll make you feel better and relieve stress at the same time. If you don't want to go to a gym, grab a friend and find a city park to walk in.

- **Girl's Night Out** -- Schedule a girl's night out with a few of your close, trusted friends. These are the girls you can vent your frustrations to about the breakup...without them judging you. These are the girls you should be able to trust to keep your deepest secrets. You'll be surprised at how much venting pent up feelings will help you through a breakup.

- **Get Your House In Order** -- Mr. Ex or Mr. Right isn't going to walk into your home, see a messy house and think, "This woman is the one for me." They don't want to bring their friends over to a pigs sty and they definitely won't want to sleep in one either. It doesn't have to be a penthouse, but clean and organized doesn't cost a cent. Make the best of what you have. Have you lived there for a year, but still have unpacked boxes? Perhaps you have ten loads of laundry that need washing. Last, but not least make sure you've removed any old photos of Mr. Ex! The old saying "Out of sight, out of mind," is true. You'll be surprised how this one little thing can remove sadness from your life quickly. Make a date with yourself to get your house in order. You'll be one-step closer to happiness and feel better about yourself once this is done.

- **Make a date with yourself to read New York Times Best Selling books** *The Rules: Time-Tested Secrets for Capturing the Heart of Mr. Right* and *The Rules II: More Rules to Live and Love By* written by Ellen Fein and Sherrie Schneider. Some of the rules are outdated, but you can modify them to make your own rules. Women all over the world use these two books like dating bibles because they work. Both books provide you with answers you need to date successfully and will show you the many mistakes you may have made with Mr. Ex. Don't worry...we've all made them.

Do whatever you have to do to make yourself feel cared for and pampered.

A girl should be two things, classy and fabulous.

COCO CHANEL

CHAPTER TEN

SKY ROCKET YOUR SELF CONFIDENCE

Think about a woman you most admire. She may be the one everyone notices. She seems to have the world in the palm of her hand. Men and women both are intrigued by her. It's not her physical beauty and bone structure people are taken with. Instead, they're intrigued by her self-confidence and the way she carries herself. Men love confident women. There's nothing sexier to the male species than a confident woman.

ARE YOU BORN WITH IT?

If you believe confidence is something you are born with...think again. Yes, there are some women that are born with it in their blood, but most have trained themselves to be confident. Train yourself to be confident and place yourself to be in a position of confidence. If you don't have it, find a way to obtain it. You've heard the old saying "Fake it till you make it?" Train and retrain yourself every day to exude confidence and watch how others react to you.

How do you train yourself to be a confident woman?

Define Yourself

Make your own rules. Know your own mind. Don't let others, society and definitely not any man dictate how you feel about yourself. Find your inner voice and set your own standards to live by. Don't let anyone's definition of his, or her own beliefs undermine your own. Write your own rules for living and develop your own standards for living. It's your life... how do you want people to think of you, or remember you? Only worry about yourself, and take care of your life, family and friends. If you're busy taking care of you, you won't give one thought, or care as to what others may, or may not think.

Define your Strengths and Know How to use them

What are you good at? What are your qualities? More importantly, what are the characteristics you love about yourself? Identify and use every one of them to your advantage. Remind yourself each day of what makes you a strong woman.

Dress the Part

Not many women like to get spruced up to run to the store to buy a loaf of bread. But if not for yourself, do it for the people you might run into while you're out running those errands. We all have bad hair days but for the love of God have some pride. If you look a mess, you'll feel like a mess. Don't show up to work with the appearance that says "I'm ready for a day at the Laundromat," (or a night at the bar). Before you leave your house each day ask yourself what your appearance says to others. If it took you only two minutes to get dressed, chances are your appearance tells others you look like hell.

Make the Most out of Life

It's easy to get into a comfort zone, which is also known as a rut. Try new things, go places you may not normally go and do things you normally wouldn't do. You never know you might actually have fun... *and meet someone new.*

Surround Yourself with Positive People and Affirmations

What are the books and magazines your read? What music do you listen to? What does your Twitter and Facebook feed look like? Replace any negatives with positives. If there are people in your life that are poison, remove them at once. Choose to read only books and articles that enrich your life. Remove toxic friends from your life. Change your mindset and the atmosphere around you with your attitude. Tell yourself every day:

I love myself.
I believe in myself.
I am capable of achieving any goal I set.
I shine.
I feel great.
I look great.
Today will be an awesome day!

Write it down, place it in a drawer you open every morning so it's the first thing you see. If you say it to yourself, you'll believe in yourself. Make a point each day to let the best of you reflect outwardly to everyone you come in contact with. With consistency you'll become the woman everyone notices.

DIVE INTO THE DATING POOL

The biggest mistake women make is by devoting all of their time and attention to one man that isn't in return devoting all of *his* time and attention to her. You may feel bad about dating more than one man, but don't. Men do this all the time. They're just experts when it comes to hiding it. Men want sex, women want security. Until a man is providing you with security along with anything else you want, don't provide him with an exclusive relationship with sex. It's that simple. If a man likes you...*really likes you*, he'll make it clear he doesn't want you to continue dating other men.

Acknowledge and understand that life as you knew it is over with Mr. Ex. You're a single woman that's free to date any man you so desire. And as long as you're not sleeping with every guy you date *(unless you want to)* it's perfectly fine to move forward dating without guilt. Keep your options open even if Mr. Ex comes back in the picture. This will give him a little reminder that he's not the only fish in the sea and makes you more attractive at the same time.

When you learn how to date several men it does nothing but sky rockets your self-confidence, because choosing who you want to spend your time becomes more like selecting the right pair of shoes for the perfect dress. It puts you back in the position of selector instead of the chaser. It fills up your calendar where you're no longer waiting on one man to call, because you have many men to keep you occupied. You change your position from needing someone, to being *wanted* by someone. Keep at least three to four men in the dating pool regardless if you like one more than the other. And until the man you're in love with slides an engagement ring on your little finger, keep your options open.

Be Mysterious --

Men love a woman that is a little elusive and hard to figure out. Why? Because it intrigues him and leaves him craving more. And after a breakup, becoming a mystery can be attractive and a challenge. If you've played by the rules and not called or text, Mr Ex will eventually call because 'curiosity kills the cat'. He'll eventually want to know what's going on in your life and more importantly, why you're not calling. When he does call let it go directly to voicemail. After the third or fourth attempt he makes, respond to one. If by phone be polite but don't offer too much information and be the first to end the conversation. If by text again be polite, but vague. And whatever you do, don't start off by telling him how much you've missed him and can't wait to see him again. If you run into him at a social function be polite and make your exit first. Again, leave him wondering and guessing where you're going and what you've been up to.

The Biggest Attraction Killer

If you want to see a man run like a professional athlete...be needy. *There's nothing more unattractive to a man than a needy, clingy woman.* A man wants to feel needed and appreciated, but he doesn't want to feel as if your life and happiness depends on him. If you notice yourself doing any of the following, realize you may have too much time on your hands and start finding ways to occupy your time.

Signs you may be acting a little too needy

- You feel the need to stay in constant contact, to know where he is at all times.

- You seek out attention.

- You constantly worry about being dumped.

- You're always available, even cancelling your own plans to be with him.

- You do whatever he wants.

- You try to make him feel guilty that he's not doing everything you want to do.

- You sulk if he doesn't give all of his attention to you

- You create drama.

Any sign of neediness, drama or desperation kills the attraction a man has for you faster than turning off a light switch. It screams *"Something is wrong with me!"* The same is true for a woman who allows a man to walk on her like a treadmill. Men don't find doormats or pushovers attractive. Know your value and understand the qualities you bring to a relationship. Show him that you are a woman of substance.

He's so lucky to be going out with me.

KATE MIDDLETON

CHAPTER ELEVEN

HOW TO MAKE MR. EX MISS YOU

Helen Rowland once said, "A man is like a cat; chase him and he will run. Sit still and ignore him and he'll come purring at your feet." It's really that simple. We as women make it complicated because it goes against every fiber of our being to ignore someone. We think it's rude, or assume a man will think we're being mean if we don't respond.

Think about how you feel when you're being ignored. You immediately panic and start to worry you've done something wrong. And that's exactly what he'll do if you push his emotional hot buttons. It shatters his fragile ego. And don't think that because you don't return a phone call, or ignore a text it will deter his efforts. The harder it is to win you over the more exhilarating the victory is for him in the end.

By giving Mr. Ex space, and more importantly silence...you transfer those feelings of loss, rejection and abandonment that he placed on you, right back to him. Often men fail to realize what they have until it is gone and it's your job to make him realize what he's lost.

As I mentioned before, after a breakup Mr. Ex is expecting you to call him crying, drowning in your sorrows, in a state of depression, groveling and pleading with him to take you back. He's expecting the drama show you provide to be better than the Super bowl half time entertainment. When you do the exact opposite of what he's expecting it throws a kink in his rope and he'll soon begin to second-guess himself. He thinks, "Wait. What just happened? Shouldn't she be calling by now?" A top-notch man wants a top notch woman that can handle her emotions and when you demonstrate you can handle your emotions you become the woman with the Midas touch.

Only when you go silent and *ignore* him will he begin to wonder what you're doing. Think back to the thoughts going through your mind. Do you wonder what he's doing? With whom is he doing it with? He'll begin to ask himself the same questions if you give him a chance.

Only when you keep your distance and avoid him at all costs will he begin to migrate back to you, but first you have to be patient and give him time to get that place. And he will never miss you, if you are constantly in his face, or trying to stay in touch with him.

Nor will he have the opportunity to wonder why you are not calling, working your fingers to the bone dialing his number in an effort to salvage the tattered relationship. Mr. Ex's imagination will go wild when he starts to think about those fingers dialing another man digits. He will begin to believe you have moved on and start to ask himself if you ever had feelings for him to begin with.

When you *respond* to calls and text messages from Mr. Ex after a breakup, you are giving him attention that feeds his fragile ego. When you give him attention, you believe it is the right thing to do, because it feels good to hear his voice and it gives him attention, which is what a woman likes. It makes *you* feel wanted because he is still keeping the lines of communication open. But it does exactly the opposite for men.

When you give Mr. Ex attention after a breakup it's simply too much, too soon. You'll never hear a man say, "I broke up with my girlfriend last week, but since then she's been really sweet. She calls and texts me throughout the day to let me know she cares, and just today I received a dozen long stem red roses. She even offered to come by and clean my house. I think I made a mistake and should give her another chance." No… he'll run faster than a gazelle with a lion on its tail *(after you have cleaned his house) and* he'll mentally file you under 'psychotic and obsessed.'

On the other hand when you go silent and let calls go directly to voicemail, he gets interested again because you appear to be a bit out of reach and more of a challenge. And a challenge triggers the attraction mechanism in the alpha male. They just cannot say *no* to a challenge…It's not in their DNA.

That's when Mr. Ex says, "I don't want to lose her, so I'd better do something before some other man does." The more he is unable to read your emotions the harder he will try and the more he will want you.

When to Respond to Mr. Ex

For every three to four attempts he makes to contact you only reply to one. No need to mention the breakup and or how lousy you are feeling. Keep the conversation light and breezy and be the first one to end the conversation. Try to keep conversations by phone to no more than five minutes. Remember that hard conversations are meant to take place face to face and if he's not verbally planning a time when he can find out what he has to do to make your relationship work, then go back to *no contact*. Only when he's making plans to see you and his actions are proving his love for you should you begin to show signs of interest again.

If you're giving too much

Take a step back by throwing all of your time, effort and attention into work, hobbies and making dates with yourself and others to keep busy. Have plans set a week in advance. Every Sunday, sit down and plan the week ahead. Even if your plan is with a DVD the couch and wearing nothing more than your pajamas. You'll look forward to it when you plan for it.

Each passing day the urge to contact him will become less of a chore and more of an accomplishment. Carry on with your life as you did prior to meeting him and prove to him (and yourself) that you're independent and perfectly capable of having a life of your own. A woman in control of her emotions appeals to a man. Men want you to depend on them and that's fine if he's doing his part, but remember he has to prove to you he can be depended on. You'll earn his respect if you raise the bar and set your standards high.

It takes four to eight weeks for a man to really experience the absence of your presence and realize that he may lose you for good. At the beginning of a breakup it's an understandable impulse for women to want to find out what went wrong, but know that most men agree that you shouldn't do a thing to get their attention. They will also tell you that you should cease all contact to shake things up a bit. So do exactly the opposite of what you want to do. This is why it's essential for you to completely break off contact. You have to take time to think with a clear head. If you don't give him the opportunity to experience what life is like without you, and make him believe you've moved on, he'll never come back to you.

TO BE ON MR. EX'S MIND

You have to make him think of you constantly. Just as playing hard to get, or actually *being hard to get* (which is much better) created an intense attraction between the two of you in the beginning, it will do the same now.

Give a little and then pull back. Carry on with your life as if there were no interruption. Don't worry he'll believe you're not interested and then be gone for good. Have faith in yourself that you're worth the effort. If a man gives up on love that easily then he wasn't really worth your time to begin with.

When you keep him guessing, it keeps him interested. Men want to win at all costs, which is exactly why they go to war, train for four years to compete in the Olympics and travel hundreds of miles only to wake up at 4 a.m. to hunt for four legged animals in freezing cold weather. So if he values you enough, the strong alpha male will hang in there for the long haul and will be thrilled when you do respond.

When he broke up with you, you may have showed all of your cards by overwhelming him with your emotional state of mind. You might have interrogated him, shown your anger or frustration and as result he shut you out. In order to make him believe he was wrong and question his judgment for breaking up with you, your only course of action to take is to go silent and *ignore him*. Redirect all the attention you were giving him, back to you. Understand there are simply no words that will work at this point. You have to reverse the roles you both were playing. And remember, the happiest relationships come from the man being the pursuer.

When you take a "vow" of silence, cease initiating any form of communication and don't respond to his attempts... that's when he begins to miss you, long for you and want you back in his life.

Think about Kate Middleton. After patiently waiting for years for Prince William to propose, he broke up with her. Can you imagine her devastation? Reports were that she was beside herself with grief. Privately I'll bet she went to pieces, but publicly she never looked better. Within a month after the breakup she began working out and got in the best shape of her life. She became a social butterfly hosting charity events and was seen out and about enjoying the nightlife. Look at where that got her.

You may not have photographers waiting to snap pictures of your every move, but you do have the power of social media... *Use it wisely*.

———————

A sure way to lose happiness, I found, is to want it at the expense of everything else.

BETTY DAVIS

———————

CHAPTER TWELVE

WHAT YOU SHOULD DO TO GET HIM BACK

Sarah Jessica Parker once said, "When men attempt bold gestures generally it's considered romantic. When women do it, it's often considered desperate or psycho." The best approach is to not take an approach at all. *Yes, that's right,* your only job is to sit back and be the soft, sweet, feminine creature God made you to be.

A man's purpose is to pursue you, protect you and at his core he *wants* to make you happy. To do otherwise is stealing the thrill of the chase from him. Women that know their worth won't make any effort whatsoever to gain the interest of a man. They have more of a *take it or leave it* attitude. When a man realizes that he has lost a good woman he'll put forth every effort in his power to get her back. It could be that he needed time and space. It's very possible it could be another woman and if that's the case he knows that he'll have to work like hell to get back in your good graces. It's that simple. In today's modern world we often forget to be women and let the man take the lead.

Chasing a man may work out for a little while, but the happiest women understand that confidence comes from knowing he wants you. This is why the pursuit is crucial... It proves his worthiness and ultimately separates the boys from the men. And you gain confidence knowing without a doubt he's right where he wants to be. A man just doesn't appreciate a woman that's easy to get. He may keep an easy catch around for a little while, but he'll never slide a ring on her finger.

A SMART WOMAN IS A PATIENT WOMAN

Patience shows self-control and maturity, two qualities men love in a woman. It shows him that you have control over your own emotions. Focus on becoming the most amazing woman you can be. Say and repeat to yourself …. Me. Me. Me. Me. Me. It's time to show Mr. Ex and the potential Mr. Rights of the world the prize you are and put your best self forward.

During this time rediscover what it takes to make you happy and fulfilled. We all need a little tweak now and then. Now is the time to get passionate about your life. You want a man that is going to consistently make you his priority. And for whatever reason, whether it was timing, personality conflict, or another woman, you have to accept that Mr. Ex wasn't bringing what you needed to the table. And as I've mentioned before he's not the only man in the world with a pulse and penis. There are millions of hunters in the world... *and you're the prize game.*

FATAL MISTAKES YOU MAY BE MAKING

You may try to hurry this process up a bit by initiating some form of contact. Refrain from trying to expedite the process by making these mistakes:

Calling him

Texting him

Emailing him

Making plans for breakfast, lunch, dinner or cocktails.

In a loving way remind him that today would be your two year anniversary

Offer to cook his favorite meal

Send him old photographs of the two of you

Send him sentimental cards

Send him flowers

Initiate affection

Initiate sex

Remind him of special occasions you once shared together

Post or tweet about him

Post or tweet how much you love him

Post or tweet how much you miss him

Post or tweet how much you want him back

Wish him a Happy Birthday

Wish him a Merry Christmas

Wish him a Happy New Year

Do not make the mistake of giving him the impression he's on your mind. And it is safe to say if you are talking about him or doing for him, you are thinking of him.

Men don't like to talk about their feelings or emotions, which is exactly what you're trying to get him to do. Stop immediately and go silent, until he goes out of his way doing things for you to make you happy and content.

At the end of the day ask yourself if you really want a man that gives you no indication he's interested, available, reliable, stable, and responsible or that can be a good provider? All of which are the key ingredients for a successful long-term relationship.

———————

Love yourself first and everything else falls into line.
You really have to love yourself to get anything done
in this world.

LUCILLE BALL

———————

CHAPTER THIRTEEN

BE SMART WITH YOUR HEART

Keep Calm, Carry On

The most important reason to begin the *No Contact* rule is to take the time necessary you need to get your emotions under control and to allow your brain the time to catch up with your heart. You've heard the old saying "time heals all wounds."

It is only natural to be devastated after a breakup and for you to want the breaker, the one that hurt you the most to provide the very comfort you need to survive the highs and lows that you're experiencing. When you're in love with someone, you've bonded with them. Separation, anxiety and a host of other emotions during the first few weeks after a separation are completely normal.

Controlling your emotions shows an incredible amount of maturity on your part. I know you're falling apart on the inside and want to crawl into a cave, and it's perfectly fine to do just that. However, know that these feelings can be as long and drawn out as you let them be. You can choose to allow them to consume you, or *choose* to get out of that dark place quickly. Sure, you may have to force yourself to date when you don't want to, meet with friends when you feel like staying at home, but if you get out and about you'll end up having fun once you're there. I Promise!

With technology right at the tip of your fingertips it's too easy to let your emotions overwhelm you. And when dealing with matters of the heart, your first reactions are wrong. You have to resist the urge to fire off a text or an email. It's an impulse you must avoid like the plague. Recognize them for what they truly are... a sign of weakness. Just as yelling and screaming at someone is a sign of insecurity the same is true if you are incapable of controlling your impulses. Remember there will always be times in life that in order to win, you have to show you are not afraid to lose.

Love Yourself

Another key factor, which is equally important, is to realize there is an entire world waiting for you to enjoy it and live it. We, as women, believe that life is sweeter when there is a strong hand to hold or a chest to sleep on. However, relying on someone else to make you happy will never work in the long term. You truly have to love yourself before you can ask anyone else to love you. You simply can't control who comes and goes in and out of your life but you can control your reactions, happiness and contentment. We often forget that we have to be our own source of comfort and provide the stability we need before we can let Mr. Right provide it for us.

When you do love yourself that is when the planets will align in all aspects of your life. You deserve someone who will wrap you in a cocoon of love. Don't settle for less. I want you to believe with all of your heart, being alone doesn't mean you *are* alone. It means you're strong enough to handle the struggles life deals you and patient enough to wait for the perfect man to walk in your life. You're a beautiful soul with your own great personality, qualities and capabilities without Mr. Ex, or Mr. Right.

If you can acknowledge and accept men often have different feelings, wants, needs and desires that may not align with what you want right now in your own life, you will always be able to handle a breakup in classy way. It just has nothing to do with you. So allow yourself to move on. Don't hold on to the past. Just do yourself the favor of not allowing the mistakes of past relationships hinder your ability to move forward in future relationships.

There is no one that will ever take care of your needs and look after your best interests as you will. Be your biggest advocate. Take the necessary time to become happy with yourself. Envision the life you want that will make you happy and content. Make a plan to create that life for yourself. Love yourself and have enough self-respect to only accept the best that life and love have to offer.

The Best Definition of Love...

Love is patient and kind. Love is not jealous, boastful, proud, or rude. It does not demand its own way. It is not irritable, and it keeps no record of being wronged. It does not rejoice about injustice but rejoices whenever the truth wins out. Love never gives up, never loses faith, is always hopeful, and endures through every circumstance.

1 Corinthians 13

Question: I need to return a razor, toothbrush, and some personal items to Mr. Ex. Should I call or send him a text to make arrangements?

Answer: No. You need to place said items in the garbage. Personal items that can easily be replaced should be discarded. No further thought is required. Personal belongings of substantia value should be neatly packed in a boxed and shipped to his home address. No note. No card. Mr. Ex is anticipating opening said box to see a sappy love note begging him to come back to you. Deprive his ego and make him wonder what your intent was. If Mr. Ex insists on swinging by your house to pick up any items he's left at your place, tell him you'll be happy to leave a box with (neatly packed items) by your front door. No need to ring the doorbell. Make sure you're out shopping or visiting friends.

Question: I need to return his house key. Should I call, or send a text to make arrangements for delivery?
Answer: No. Place key in an envelope and mail it to him. Make any arrangements you need to get Mr. Ex that key without coming into contact with him. Don't waste your time preparing a card or note to go along with the key. If he has half of a brain, when he opens the envelope he'll know that it's his house key.

Question: I left my facial crème at his house. Should I drop by to pick it up?
Answer: Not unless you paid three-hundred dollars for it, there is a full jar and it was imported from England. Even in that case, if you can afford to buy facial cream for three-hundred dollars chances are you can afford another jar. Go to the drug store and buy more!

Question: We have children together. How do I start the no contact rule?

Answer: You don't. You have to communicate where the children are concerned. However, the children are the only topic you need to communicate about. Keep communication short, sweet and to the point.

Question: It's his birthday. Should I send him a Happy Birthday text?

Answer: No. He will remember who *did not* send him birthday wishes longer than he will remember who did.

Question: What about Christmas. Should I send him a friendly Merry Christmas text?

Answer: No. If Mr. Ex wishes you one, you should reply but only match the vibe he's sending. For example, if you receive a 'Merry Christmas' text, you would reply 'and one to you.' Wait at least three hours before replying. If he sends the text after eight o'clock in the evening wait until the next day to reply. Resume no contact.

Question: It's Valentine's Day, should I send a "Happy Valentines Text.?"

Answer: Can you only guess what my answer is? *No. No. No. No. No. No!* If he sends you two dozen roses, wait until the next day and reply with a simple "thank you." Resume no contact. You may not realize it unless you're able to look at his credit card statement, but men have been known to have a dozen roses sent to several different women.

If he asks you out on Valentine's Day for dinner that night, you have to find all your inner strength and respectfully decline. You can nicely reply "Have plans, perhaps some other time." I know this is hard to do, especially if your only plans are to sit at home alone with your dog to watch Grey's Anatomy. Know that if he really wanted to wine and dine you for Valentines he would have planned for this night well in advance.

I hope you understand my point. You shouldn't contact him in any form or fashion. The only time it's acceptable to break *No Contact* is if he's your next-door neighbor and you notice fire blazing from the windows of his house. It's perfectly acceptable to break *No Contact* at that time. *Don't get any ideas!*

BREAKUP RULES TO LIVE BY

Don't try to remain friends.

Don't initiate contact with Mr. Ex.

Don't try to change his mind, beg, plead or cry in front of him.

Don't frequent places you know he'll be.

Don't try to resolve problems by telephone or text messages. (Remember real conversations require eye contact)

Don't answer every time he calls. For every three attempts he makes only respond to one.

Don't respond to 'nothing' text messages.

Don't ask him for a date; wait for him to ask you. If he doesn't ask you, know he's not interested.

Don't agree to last minute dates. If he asks to meet that day, tell him you would love to, but can't. Make a suggestion for at least three days later, or the next week.

Don't answer the phone or texts after seven o'clock p.m.

Don't answer the phone or texts during weekends.

Don't invite him to your home or drive to his.

Don't accept last minute dates. If he's not planning dates accept he's not interested.

Don't compete with other women.

Don't date him if he doesn't meet your requirements.

Don't rush into sex.

Do get back to being the woman Mr. Ex fell in love with (only better.)

Do return items of his that need to be returned quickly (See FAQ's)

Do plan your week, a week in advance and keep occupied.

Do make a list of requirements you must have in a relationship.

Do take time to heal.

Do rely on friends during this time.

Do remember to always look your best.

Do start dating new men, regardless if you want to or not.

Do learn to love the chase.

Do love yourself ...

And always, always, always be classy!

TAKE TIME TO READ

The Rules: Time Tested Secrets for Capturing the Heart of Mr. Right
The Rules II: More Rules to Live and Love By
Why Men Love Bitches: A Woman's Guide to Holding Her Own in a Relationship
Why Men Marry Bitches: A Woman's Guide to Winning a Man's Heart
It's Called a Breakup Because It's Broken: The Smart Girl's Breakup Buddy
He's Just Not That Into You
Act Like a Lady, Think Like a Man: What Men Really Think About Love, Relationships, Intimacy and Commitment

Have you used *No Contact* to move past a relationship, or to get an ex-boyfriend back? If so, I would love to hear your story. Please write to me at: leslieannbraswell@aol.com, or you can follow me on Facebook here https://www.facebook.com/leslie.braswell

THE END.

Ignore the Guy, Get the Guy -The Art of No Contact ©Leslie Braswell

Made in the USA
Middletown, DE
03 April 2015